Kate Shelley

BOUND FOR LEGEND

Robert D. San Souci

paintings by Max Ginsburg

Dial Books for Young Readers *New York*

"Hers is a deed bound for legend . . . a story to be told
until the last order fades and the last rail rusts."
*—from the memorial tablet raised at Kate Shelley's gravesite in 1956
by The Order of Railway Conductors and Brakemen*

For Jack Shelley, with appreciation
R.D.S.S.

To my wife, Miryam, for her help and support
M.G.

Thanks to David Soman, whose suggestions helped
me to conceive the art for this book — M.G.

Published by Dial Books for Young Readers
A Division of Penguin Books USA Inc.
375 Hudson Street | New York, New York 10014

Typography by Amelia Lau Carling
Printed in Hong Kong | First Edition
1 3 5 7 9 10 8 6 4 2

Library of Congress Cataloging in Publication Data
San Souci, Robert D.
Kate Shelley: bound for legend / by Robert D. San Souci;
paintings by Max Ginsburg.—1st ed.   p.   cm.
Summary: A biography of the fifteen-year-old Iowa teenager who
helped avert a train disaster in 1881 and became a national heroine.
ISBN 0-8037-1289-8 (trade).—ISBN 0-8037-1290-1 (lib.)
1. Railroads—Iowa—Moingona—Accidents—Juvenile literature.
2. Shelley, Kate—Juvenile literature. 3. Heroines—Iowa—Biography
—Juvenile literature. [1. Shelley, Kate. 2. Heroines.
3. Railroads—Accidents.] I. Ginsburg, Max, ill. II. Title.
HE1780.5.I8S26 1995   363.12'2'092—dc20   [B]   93-20438   CIP   AC

*The art for each picture consists of an oil painting that
is color-separated and reproduced in full color.*

The publisher wishes to thank John D. (Jack) Shelley, nephew of Kate
Shelley and Emeritus Professor of Journalism and Mass Communication
at Iowa State University, for checking the facts in the book.

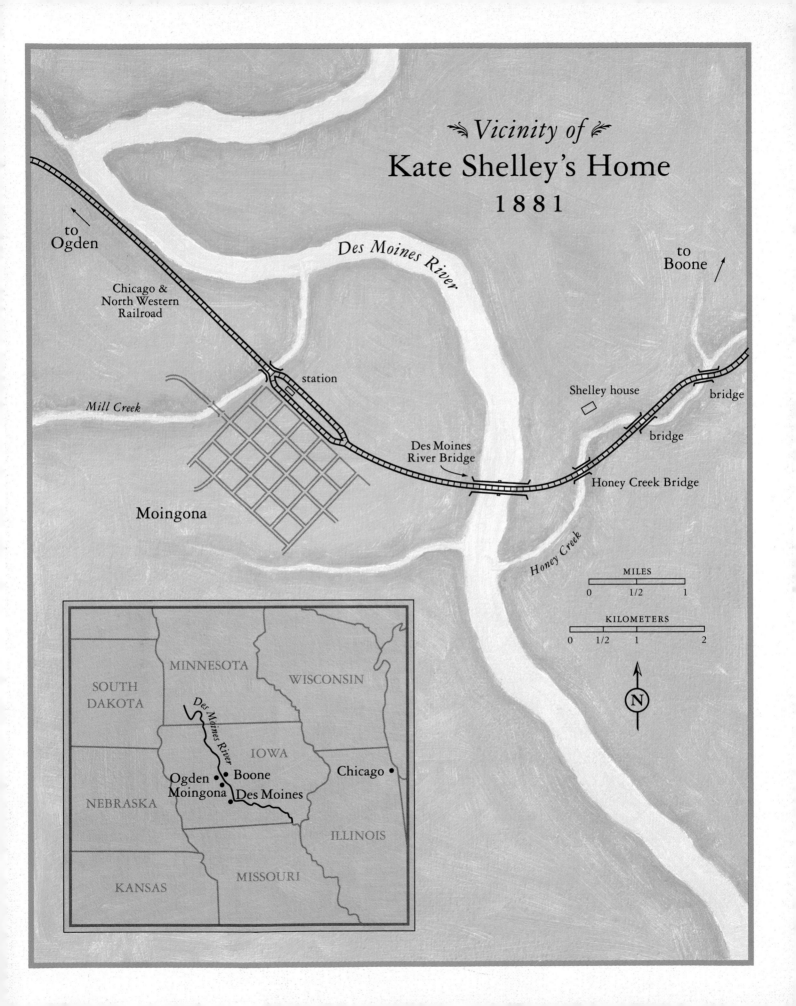

A railroad bridge crossed Honey Creek not far from
Kate Shelley's little Iowa farmhouse. Every day trains sped back and
forth over the trestle, heading east toward Chicago or west toward
the long Des Moines River Bridge on the way to Salt Lake City.
As they roared past, the trains brought a touch of excitement to
fifteen-year-old Kate's life.

Once the railroad had been the Shelley family's main source of
income. Kate's father, who had died three years earlier, had been a
section foreman on the Chicago & North Western Railway. Now,
in 1881, the farm—a patch of pasture and timber set amid rugged
hills in the heart of Iowa—supported the family.

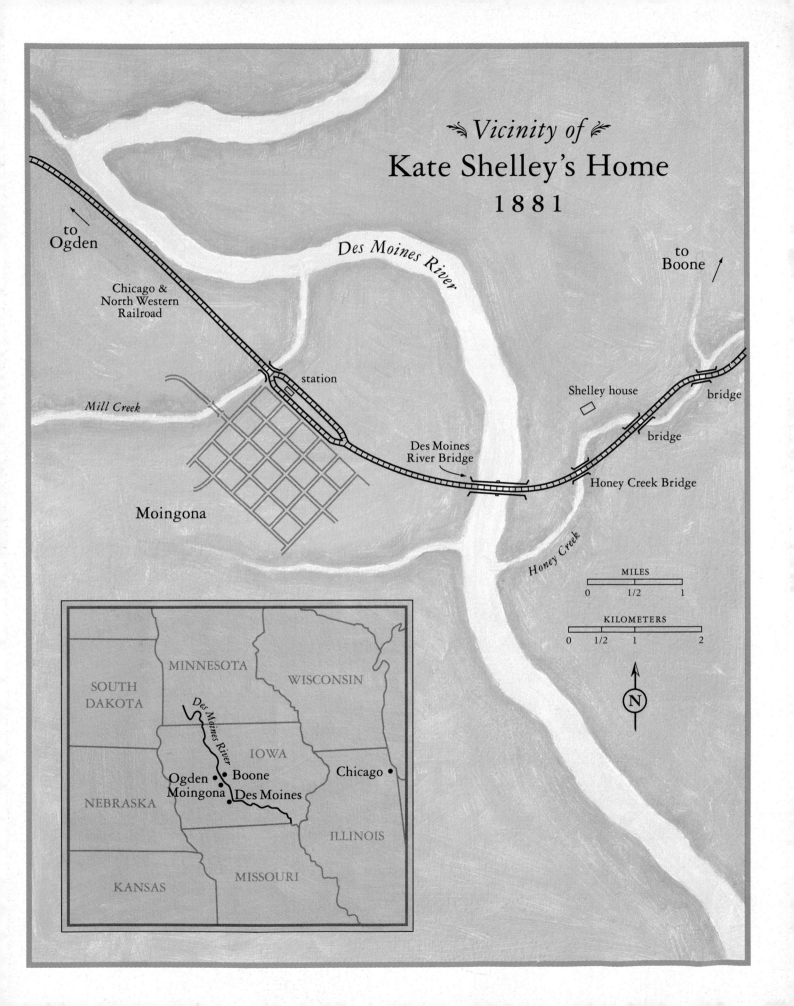

Vicinity of
Kate Shelley's Home
1881

to Ogden

to Boone

Des Moines River

Chicago & North Western Railroad

station

Shelley house

bridge

Mill Creek

Des Moines River Bridge

bridge

Honey Creek Bridge

Moingona

Honey Creek

MILES
0   1/2   1

KILOMETERS
0   1/2   1   2

N

SOUTH DAKOTA

MINNESOTA

WISCONSIN

Des Moines River

IOWA

Ogden   Boone

Moingona   Des Moines

Chicago

NEBRASKA

ILLINOIS

KANSAS   MISSOURI

A railroad bridge crossed Honey Creek not far from
Kate Shelley's little Iowa farmhouse. Every day trains sped back and
forth over the trestle, heading east toward Chicago or west toward
the long Des Moines River Bridge on the way to Salt Lake City.
As they roared past, the trains brought a touch of excitement to
fifteen-year-old Kate's life.

Once the railroad had been the Shelley family's main source of
income. Kate's father, who had died three years earlier, had been a
section foreman on the Chicago & North Western Railway. Now,
in 1881, the farm—a patch of pasture and timber set amid rugged
hills in the heart of Iowa—supported the family.

Good-natured, sturdy Kate had taken charge of the family because of her mother's poor health. She helped with the plowing and planting. With her nine-year-old sister Mayme she gathered firewood and tended the vegetable garden. She even taught herself to shoot to keep hawks away from the chickens.

Kate saw the younger children, Margaret, Mayme, and John, off to school in the morning and helped tuck them in at night. She kept them away from the dangerous banks of Honey Creek, because none of them could swim. One brother, James, had drowned shortly after his father's death. Kate was the one who discovered his riderless horse beside the Des Moines River, where the boy had been swept away while wading.

In moments between chores Kate read every book she could lay her hands on, to make up for her lack of schooling. She loved to ride bareback through the forests in autumn or row a skiff along the broad, smooth surface of the river in high summer.

But the railroad was her real love. When errands took her to the little coal mining village of Moingona, a mile away, she would stop by the train station. She would linger in the waiting room with its potbellied stove and high-backed bench. Sometimes she would hear urgent tapping from behind the ticket window as news came over the telegraph wire, or as the stationmaster sent word to distant stations to alert approaching trains of hazards.

Adventure appealed to Kate. "She was absolutely without fear," her sister Mayme would recall later in life. But her adventures were confined to farm and family for the first fifteen years of her life— until one July day in 1881.

When the eastbound freight from Moingona neared the Shelley farm on the afternoon of Wednesday, July 6, 1881, Kate and her mother were taking the wash off the clothesline. It had rained for most of a week, and now black clouds were heaping up on the horizon, threatening another storm. But Kate stopped pulling sheets, shifts, and stockings from the line long enough to watch Engine 230 help a freight train climb the grade up to Honey Creek Bridge on its way to Boone, a town five miles distant.

The freight train was late. Kate knew the schedules by heart, and she could recognize each of the local "pushers" (Number 230 was one) by its whistle. These four locomotives sat on sidetracks until they were needed to help push or pull heavy trains up the steep slope.

As Mrs. Shelley and Kate lifted the full laundry basket, the sky went dark as if a black curtain had been flung across the sun. They barely reached the back door of their two-story clapboard house before the first heavy rain-drops began to fall.

Soon the deadly storm broke. "You can only imagine what a fearful thing it is to see the heavens grow black and blacker until the light of day is all shut out," Kate later said, "to see the clouds torn into fragments by the fierce lightnings, and the torrents fall and swallow up the earth."

Thunder rattled loose glass in the window frame, while fierce wind

hurled sheets of rain against the house. Kate watched anxiously as
Honey Creek's waters rose higher than she had ever seen them.

   She soon began to fear for the safety of the animals in the barn on
the slope below the house. Putting on an old coat and hat, she hurried
to the barn through the ankle-deep water gushing down the hillside.

The water was just as deep inside. The plow horses, cattle, and hogs were splashing nervously in their stalls and pens. Kate led each of them to higher ground in an oat field, then turned them loose.

By the time she returned to the barn for a last look around, the water had grown knee-deep. Hearing a terrified squealing, Kate discovered several piglets that had climbed onto an island of hay. She carried them to the safety of the oat field and tucked them under the sow. Then, drenched and chilled, she ran back to the house.

As she dried off by the kitchen stove, Kate heard the frightening noise of trees being uprooted by the gale. The younger children were fed and put to bed, but the effort didn't take Kate's mind off raging Honey Creek. With every lull in the downpour, Kate saw picket fences, parts of walls, even small trees pile up against the straining supports of the trestle over the brimming stream.

As Kate noted the passing hours, she began to worry about the midnight express. "Surely no trains will be dispatched in this storm," Margaret Shelley said to soothe her daughter.

It was well past eleven o'clock when Kate clearly heard the rumble of a pusher engine climbing the grade to Honey Creek Bridge. She heard its bell clang twice. Then there was a dreadful crash, followed by an awful hiss of steam as hot metal hit cold water.

"Oh, Mother!" cried Kate, clutching Margaret's hand. "It's Number Eleven. They've gone down Honey Creek Bridge!"

For a moment the two stared at each other in horror, while Mayme, awakened by the sound, huddled in the kitchen door. Then Kate reached for her damp coat and soggy straw hat hanging beside the stove. "I must go to help the men," Kate said.

Mrs. Shelley begged her not to go, but Kate insisted. "If that were Father down there," she said, "we'd expect someone to help him." Then, mindful of a graver danger, she added, "And I must stop the midnight train from the west."

Hundreds of passengers bound for Chicago would be aboard the express train headed for the ruined Honey Creek Bridge. Kate told her mother that she would go to Moingona Station and have the station-master telegraph a warning down the line. If she couldn't reach the station in time, she would flag down the train herself.

Quickly she took her father's old railroad lantern and filled it with oil. There was no wick, so Kate grabbed an old flannel skirt and tore off a strip. In a moment she had lit the lamp.

"Kate, if you go out there, you'll be lost or hurt," her mother said in a last effort to make her stay.

"I could never forgive myself if I didn't," she replied.

Her mother sighed. "Go, then, in the name of God, and do what you can."

Because the front yard was flooded, Kate followed a path that led up the slope behind the house, then veered toward the shattered trestle. Her mother suddenly ran after Kate, but slipped in the water streaming down the hillside. Kate helped her to her feet, saw that she was all right, then continued on her way. While Mayme stared from the window, Mrs. Shelley paced back and forth in the mud and water, keeping a frantic watch on Kate.

Kate slogged through the rain until she came to the bluff above Honey Creek. From this twenty-foot drop-off, Honey Creek Bridge had once extended across to the facing bluff. Amid the broken timbers and pilings a small rounded section of the steam engine jutted out of the churning black water. Only a bit of railing marked the sunken "tender," the special car that carried water and coal for the engine. The unfortunate crew had been sent out to check for storm-damaged tracks. Kate would later learn that two men aboard the locomotive had been killed.

Moving along the cliff, Kate waved her lantern. In response two men shouted up to her. She could barely see them as they clung to some willow branches above the raging water. She called back to them, and they yelled something up to her. But the storm was so fierce that she couldn't make out what they said.

Kate realized that she could do nothing for them by herself, and time was running out for the midnight express. She turned and headed for the Des Moines River Bridge. Moingona Station and its telegraph were on the other side.

Kate struggled on against the pelting rain as bushes and brambles snagged her clothes. The lightning seemed a hundred times more frightening in the open, but it lit the long bridge that was her goal.

Inch by inch, Kate fought her way up the steep approach to the bridge. Though the span was normally a full fifty feet above the water, the angry river seemed only a short distance below her. Before she reached the bridge, the wind extinguished her feeble lamp, and she had no way to relight it.

Fearfully she peered into the dark, afraid that the midnight express might be speeding across the bridge. But no whistle knifed through the howling wind; no engine's headlamp hurtled toward her.

Nearly seven hundred feet long, the Des Moines River Bridge was a ladder of cross ties, each nearly two feet apart. Though Kate had crossed the bridge in good weather, its splintery ties were studded with twisted spikes and nails to discourage such foot traffic.

"Those who cross a railroad bridge on a swiftly moving train can form no conception of the sensation a traveler experiences who attempts to cross on foot," Kate later said. "A misstep would send me down

below the ties into the flood that was boiling below. I got down on
my hands and knees, carrying yet my useless lantern and guiding
myself by the stretch of rail."

Shivering from the wet and cold, Kate crept along, avoiding the
worst buffeting of the wind. She would reach her fingers out to locate
the next tie, then cross to it with the help of the iron track. Again and
again, her skirt or coat sleeve caught on a nail or spike or splinter. Her
hands and knees were cut and bleeding. Several times she nearly lost
her hold on the rain-slick ties. The hungry river was terrifying to Kate,
who was near the spot where her brother James had drowned.

"Halfway over, a piercing flash of lightning showed me the angry flood more closely than ever," Kate would remember, "and swept along upon it a great tree—the earth still hanging to its roots—was racing for the bridge, and, it seemed, for the very spot I stood upon. Fear brought me upright on my knees, and I clasped my hands in terror, and in prayer, I hope, lest the shock should carry out the bridge."

Kate braced for the crash. But the huge tree swept between the pilings, its branches grabbing and slapping at her through the ties. She was spattered with water and foam from the snapping limbs before the raging waters swept the tree into the darkness downriver.

Without her lantern Kate knew she had no hope of flagging down the midnight express. She had to reach Moingona Station so that a warning could be sent.

So tired that she could only think of reaching the next tie, and then the next, Kate began to crawl the rest of the way across the bridge. The cold numbed the stinging in her hands and knees. Raising her head, she took heart when she saw the lights of the railway station in the distance.

At last she reached solid ground. She paused just long enough to catch her breath. Then, forcing herself to her feet, she ran the half mile remaining to Moingona Station.

She burst into the waiting room, where several men were talking, and blurted out her warning. Kate later admitted that she had no memory of how, exactly, she told her tale. She only remembered someone saying, "The girl is crazy."

But the station agent cried, "That's Kate Shelley! She would know if the bridge was out!"

Then Kate, exhausted by her ordeal, collapsed on the spot.

When she came to a few moments later, she was lying on the hard, cold wooden bench. To her relief she found that the midnight express had not yet come through.

Much later she would learn that the train had been halted forty miles to the west, at the edge of the storm. The passengers were safe, but other lives were still in danger.

"The crew from Number Eleven still need help," Kate said. She quickly agreed to guide the rescue mission to save the men. Though others tried to get her to rest, Kate would not be put off.

Engine 230, sidetracked in the Moingona Station yard, was quickly filled with volunteers carrying ropes and shovels. As it headed for the fallen trestle, the engineer kept sounding the whistle to let the stranded men know that help was on the way.

Riding in the cab, Kate must have held her breath as the train eased across the Des Moines Bridge. But the structure proved solid, and the storm was quieting at last.

Exhausted yet determined, Kate guided the others to where she had seen the two crewmen in Honey Creek. The men, Number Eleven's engineer and brakeman, still clung to branches above the receding water, but there was no way for the rescuers to get down to the stream. Kate had to lead them into the hills behind her home—reversing the path she had traced earlier that evening—to an undamaged railroad bridge beyond the house.

Only now could they follow the track back west to reach the stranded men. By the time they were brought to safety, the rain had almost ceased, and chilly gray dawn had begun to lighten the sky.

Shaking from cold and weariness, Kate was brought home. Her mother hugged her, then put her to bed, mounding the blankets above the shivering girl.

The story of Kate's bravery was telegraphed all over the state and across the nation. She was celebrated in countless newspapers as "the Iowa heroine."

But Kate was too sick to care. Over and over she repeated to Mayme, "I can still feel the cold rain on my face."

At one point her teeth began to chatter so loudly that Mrs. Shelley was forced to send for the doctor; but all he could do was whittle a peg from soft wood. He told Kate's mother, "Put this between her teeth to keep her from breaking them."

Strangers gathered in the yard to look at "Our Kate," as they called her. Some even asked for a bit of her skirt or a lock of her hair. Mrs. Shelley shooed them away.

It was nearly three months before Kate's strength came back. During this time as she lay in bed, she was greeted by the trains that blew their whistles when they passed the Shelley farmhouse.

Finally, one afternoon she announced that she felt well enough to go outside. Escorted by her mother, sisters, and brother, Kate stepped out on the porch, hoping to catch a glimpse of the westbound train. To her surprise, the train stopped in front of the house, and crew and passengers leaned out to cheer her. Red-faced but delighted, she waved back to them.

Later, when she was able to go into town, the trains would stop and carry her to Moingona.

Many honors came to Kate in the days that followed. She received a medal from the state of Iowa, inscribed:

Presented by the State of Iowa, to Kate Shelley,
with the thanks of the General Assembly
in recognition of the Courage and Devotion
of a child of fifteen years whom neither the fury of the elements,
nor the fear of death could appall in her effort to save human life
during the terrible storm and flood in the Des Moines Valley
on the night of July 6th, 1881.

There were other gifts and awards, but perhaps the most wonderful for Kate was a lifetime pass on the railroad. In the years that followed she attended Simpson College, and in 1903 became station agent at Moingona. She held this job until illness forced her to retire in 1911. She died the following year at the age of forty-six.

Always modest when asked about her heroic deed, Kate would say, "I believe that God makes strong the weakest and makes the poorest of us able to do much for His merciful purposes."

Kate's final train ride came on the day of her funeral. A special train stopped at the Shelley home to pick up her coffin and carry her to the Boone depot. Her resting place was the Sacred Heart Cemetery on the edge of Boone.

Author's Note

This story draws upon the wealth of Kate Shelley materials preserved in the archives of the Ericson Public Library in Boone, Iowa. These include the first newspaper accounts of the disaster; numerous articles from newspapers, magazines, and journals; Kate's and Mayme's own recollections; and much more. An exhibit room at the Boone County Historical Society Museum features much additional Kate Shelley memorabilia, including the medal awarded to Kate by the Iowa General Assembly and the lantern she carried. The Historical Society also operates the Kate Shelley Memorial Park and Railroad Museum on the spot where the Moingona station was located in 1881.

Of particular help was the detailed account, "The Girl They Stopped the Trains For: The *True* Story of Kate Shelley" by Edward H. Meyers, published in *Trains* magazine in October 1957. Mayme Shelley commented about this story, "In my estimation it is as nearly accurate an account as has been written," while Jack Shelley, Kate's nephew, also strongly endorses the article. Meyers's account points out that, though Kate didn't know it at the time, the railroad had stopped all freight and passenger trains in either direction at the edge of the storm.

I hope readers will agree that this fact in no way diminishes Kate's courageous efforts. To the best of her knowledge, the midnight express was rushing headlong toward disaster—and her prompt action undeniably saved the lives of the two men trapped by the floodwaters of Honey Creek.

The Kate Shelley High Bridge, opened to train traffic in 1901, spans the Des Moines River Valley not far from the site of Kate's heroic deed. It is still one of the longest and highest double-track railroad bridges in existence.